# The Last Day on Earth

J Henderson

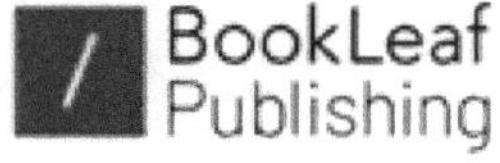

BookLeaf Publishing

Presentation by *BookLeaf Publishing*

Web: www.bookleafpub.com

E-mail: info@bookleafpub.com

ISBN: 9789357210836

First edition 2022

# DEDICATION

For Mum

# ACKNOWLEDGEMENT

Many thanks to those who have made my recovery possible and to those who support me every day to find who I am and be content.

# The Last Day on Earth

The last day on Earth I walked to heaven
Stoned and alone, I walked forever,
Not following the limits of the curb,
Or the rain and weather,
The rain from heaven,

The Sun won't reach me, and The Sun won't
burn me
The stars have gone cold, and we're no longer
turning,

I never stopped walking, I never started
crawling,
I never stopped, I never slowed, I never stopped
falling,

The last day on Earth I had to be high
Stoned and alone, I was trying to die,
Treading, not following the limits of the sky,
Dreading returning home alive,

God won't touch me, nobody will,
Alone, I'm growing, in the dark I'm growing,
In the shadows on Earth, by heaven
I'm toing and froing on the edge of life

The deepest darkness, where I dwell,
A bridge to peace, away from hell.

# The Voice

I'm the shadow in the window
The one that you know
The ghost in the background
The empty, troubled soul
I'm the wind in your bedroom
When the door's closed
I'm the voice behind your ear
When you are alone.

# Stranger

I'm a stranger, on all fours
I get stranger behind closed doors
Behind broken laws, I'm the strangest
Floating against gravity, up into space
Soaring into agony, towards cold embraces
Drawing a fantasy, I hope it's persuasive
I'm filled with anxiety, just look at my paintings
Haunted by substances,
Taunted by voices,
I'm met with impatience, guarding all your
secrets
I'm an inpatient, harbouring all these cuts,
Rising from the pavement, defying physics
I'm completely vacant, my spirit is rigid
I can't move, I can't move
I can't see, I can't see
There's just me, and a thousand voices
I'm lonely, and there's too many noises
Watch closely, I'm making bad choices
I can't move, I can't see
A thousand pairs of eyes are watching me.

# Hospital

Memories and thoughts of a dark place
Clinical white walls with perpetual shade
From freedom to incarcerated disgrace
Where identities and voices continue to fade
A confusing and confined space
Where new traumas are made,

And new friendships are made
With a mutual understanding
Our lives will never be the same
Our feet are all landing in the same grave
A place where I'm glad I came
Despite the misery, despite the pain.

# Pill Voice

I can't remember my life
I can't remember today
I was born in the cold, out in the rain
In the midst of thick smoke
I was born in the night
My eyes were closed
I was born without light

I can't remember the times before I knew God
Who shone the light in my eyes,
And gave me a job
Gave me the power to see
But all I see is wrong
And when I try to perceive
I cannot see beyond
I only see within
The body is a shell
I only hear within
The Other will tell
There's hands and there's eyes under my skin
and they tell me something
They show me myself

They have me rolled up,

Like a cigarette
And I'm willed to shut up
I'm willed to forget
But I've stayed silent for too fucking long
Fuck hiding the truth, the truth is all gone
Fuck hiding the truth, the truth is all wrong.

# Snow

Clutching the spoon with a rusted vice
Blue lips, cheeks drained of blood
Staring at the moon with empty eyes
Tulips bleak, shrivelled at the bud
Gasping for breath, out of instinct
Liquid death in the cracks of the wood
Naked trees shivering in the breeze
Night birds sinking into the foot
Of snow, upon the frozen grass
Their beaks reach down below
Ragged denim clinging to a mass
Faded ink within unwashed skin
Fading in and out of the night
Yellow thumbs reach the flint
To sap strength out of sight.

# True Colours

Golden lights,
Angelic life,
Blue-lipped, blue-tinged skin
Yellow is sin,
Blue is right,
Red-messaged with black sight
True colours on a truthful night

Bruised body, bruised mind,
A used discovery, used insight
Inside, numb, outside, no fight
Left unscrewed, loose not tight

# Blood

In one smooth motion
The dangerous act goes forth
Rushing pain through blood

The torn open flesh
Oozes blood and sets alight
Crimson flames of pain

Mysterious air
Wind obscuring shadows hide
Cool and collected

Eyes burning with rage
Kicking an orange around
For the hell of it

The door left open
The entrance inviting all
The bubbling tar roads.

# The Husky

Tired and low, the husky glides across the
pavement
No one sees him, no one except me
He veers down Sackville Street, unalive and
unknown
Paws sliding across battered concrete
Nose inhaling distant memories, sniffing intently
Abandoned eyes piercing the veil of night
Following dreams into cyclical depression
Following dreams into an insanity
The husky hides in the shadows of paranoia
He raises his nose to the morning scent
He pulls on the leash, with great yellow teeth
And wags his tail, so innocent,
So soft and harmless, so strong and free
The dog is a monster, the dog has a lead
For everyone, for you and for me.

# Sunshine

Sunshine can make beauty of a terrible day
Sunshine can magnify the smallest grace
Lemon-hued leaves and sun-smelling skin
Grateful green trees and a wild garlic hint
Vast rolling fields of viridescence and mint
Aching blue sky, stretching so wide
Making you high, on life's small gifts
Sunshine sets alight the stunning morning,
Sunshine can fight the battle of night
On cold shivering shoulders,
In squinting brown eyes
Sunshine is beautiful and this is all why.

# Happy Birthday

Happy birthday to the most unhappy
Lying in a haram grave
Unbeknownst and tragic
Lying in a cool dark cave
Just waiting for the stone to roll away
Was it in a bag, or was it rope?
Was it alcoholic black or was it dope?
Irretrievable disappointment
Unforgivable same old
Distancing despite apologies
This bad thing, not a quality
I forgive you, I forgive you
There was no grave mistake
There was no ill-intention
But irretrievable disappointment
It's incurable and hard to take
A poet, I should mention
Characterised by avoidance,
I should just poison, myself
For my error, for my immaturity
There was never a promise
Of security,
Smoked away friendships
Undone shoelaces
I remember you, I remember you

There was no evil inside you
There was no hate from you
It wasn't 'cause of people,
Or 'cause I denied the truth
It is what it is because it was inevitable
No, it was avoidable
It was a choice from you.

# Comfort

When you go away to wherever you've gone,
I am here, walking the dog, knitting on the sofa
and dancing in the kitchen while making the tea.
A little sadder because I'm never sure where you
are,
but I smile because I know you'll come back to
me.

When you come back, confused and sleepy,
ready for my love,
I am here, walking the dog, knitting on the sofa
and dancing in the kitchen while making your
tea.
I smile to welcome you back, a little sadder
inside because you left something behind.

# Why delay the inevitable?

Why delay the inevitable
Why live at all
Why survive, when I will die,
Why hide the feelings, the truths,
The lies,
Why pretend I'm alive,
The mind knows it's dying,
And the soul knows it's dead,
Gone, already, the head a mere shell,
This is darkness,
This is life, nearly death, where I dwell.

Why numb the pain
When it will always come back
From life to life
It stalks, it chases, it attacks,
From soul to soul
The sane don't suffer,
They say we're ill, depressed, those fuckers,
We stress, we suffer, we see,
Yet we must try to be blind
For the sake of sanity, her
Invisible face, she's so unkind.

Cleanse my mind of the truth

Fill me with false memories,
Forced smiles, fake hope, drill holes in my skull,
And inject me with faith
Faith and strength so I can pull
Myself from the deep, to
To stand at the side, to
Be comfortable, and at ease,
To be healthy, sober, to have peace,
But I don't need that for me
The deep is where I belong,
It's what I need, the darkness,
Where I already grew strong, I did suffer,
But I need that for me,
I need the struggle, to fight to breathe,
I need the panic, the rush, the fear, the lust,
I want the high, but for that I need the low,
The lowest I can get, I crawl and crawl,
I never stop, I never slow,
The steady suffer, it grows me,
I'm addicted, it kills me,
The truth is that
I'm addicted to killing me

# Untitled

Incarcerate me
I'm fine without you
Just don't take my book
Don't take my pencil away
Flagellate me
I'm fine with the pain
Just don't give that look
Don't take my friend away
Criticise me
I know I can take it
Don't hold back
Don't take my breath away
Summer is cold and the winter is warm
The Earth has stopped orbiting
Ahead is coming the storm
Our rights are fading in the confused seasons
Free all the prisoners, free the religions, free all
the sufferers
We don't have control
It's out of our hands, it's beyond our grasp
Certainty we don't deserve, it's too much to ask
What happens when the star engulfs the world?
When death knocks us down?
Incarcerate me, for telling the truth
Flagellate me, for being no use

Criticise me, I've nothing to lose

# Suburbs

Green glowing hedges, open doorway
Where two tupsels sat
On the doorstep with wooden fingers
And smokeless cigarettes burning into curling
ash
The concrete quarter pipe
Vandalised with pleasure
And randomised traffic lights
Amber, red, green, spark and explode
Like the sick-minded pink-pounded writer
With his wiry spine protruding through skin
Abandoned buildings on bending backstreets
Faceless
Controlling vocal emotions, inanimate facade
Feelingless staring
Through middle class bay windows and
Electrified front pockets
Glimmering sunlit pylons
Encrypted love songs, messages
From one transmission tower
To another, uniformed architecture
And the rocking of the train
With no destination, drawing a pattern
Through fields of waves and bony fish
Afaded sunglow, midnight approaches.

# The Pain-Pleasure Cycle

The pain-pleasure cycle jerks into motion
Opium too potent, meconium,
broken open inside the immature seed home,
can't wait 'til it's frozen,
it's too late, he's starting to feel emotion
The seeds are chosen, golden tea and liquid,
Like celestial juice drained from a star, wicked,
Evil pain-pleasure drawing animals from men,
Don't snap the stem, death starts to tempt,
The rent's due but he has to have a tenth, again,
And again when will this end?

# Summer

Electric cars silently glide into decorated
driveways
Pebble pools bake in the staring sun
Red-brick facades glow and deflect
Outside accusations and middle class fear
Pain-pleasure stench drifts across the valley
The smooth, glistening canal oozes East
Little toy dogs prance across polished
pavements
Their tiny paws sinking into unhappy marriages
and
Stolen newborn's first steps, towards insanity
Well-behaved birds swoop down to milk bottle
tops
Clutching the prize with elegant talons
Soaring into summer jets, holidaygoers witness
Bird murder, no justice for life when it is
summer.

# An Early Thought

An early thought
Old like ochre
Yellow and brown
Caught like a photo
Framed and bought
Clean and sober
Mellow and drowned
Complex composure
Slow until it's over
Quickly zipped up
Robbed of closure
Closed, hung over a shoulder
Closed, eyes glazed over.

# Untitled

Cracked weed-ridden pavement
And substance enslavement
Cracked teeth and payment
Coins split in irous desperation
Muralled walls, inside the basement
Inside the tea rooms, fragrant
Inside his stare, vacant
When am I getting out?
This minute has been ages
I'm a voiceless patient
I'm voiceless and impatient
Sick of days without changes
Sick of flat vocal ranges